EVERYDAY AFFIRMATIONS

365 days of thought-provoking, daily affirmations and journal prompts

from the author of,
"Mastering the Art of Internal Intimacy"

DEVYN PENNEY

BALBOA.PRESS
A DIVISION OF HAY HOUSE

Balboa Press books may be ordered through booksellers or by contacting:

Balboa Press
A Division of Hay House
1663 Liberty Drive
Bloomington, IN 47403
www.balboapress.com
844-682-1282

Cover by FORGETYOUSAWIT

Print information available on the last page.

ISBN: 979-8-7652-3299-6 (sc)
ISBN: 979-8-7652-3300-9 (hc)
ISBN: 979-8-7652-3301-6 (e)

Balboa Press rev. date: 08/23/2022

this book is dedicated to you.

A few minutes is all it takes to incorporate mindfulness and intention into your daily routine. With 365 daily thoughts, affirmations, and prompts, "Everyday Affirmations" helps you start every day with conscious, inner dialogue and optimism. An affirmation is anything you say out loud or think to yourself. We may not always realize it, but a lot of what we usually say and think is more negative than positive. The problem with negative words and thought patterns is that they determine our reality.

Negative thoughts equal negative experiences. Our words carry a vibration sent out into the world and bounced back to us; negative words emit a low vibration, which means that negative energy is always sent back to you. Our brain believes what we tell it, whether real or imagined, so why not tell it that we are who we want to be? We must re-teach our brains to think positively about ourselves and the world around us. Psychology Today writes, "After being studied extensively by social psychologists, self-affirmation has now just begun to receive attention. Repeated use of affirmations in a meditative state can help rewrite brain messages".

By going from negative thoughts to consistent, repetitive, positive thoughts, your brain chemistry will change, and so will your life. I discovered the power of affirmations years ago and have never looked back. I am confident that when you see radical improvement in your daily life, neither will you. Coupling positive affirmations with prompted journaling on the subject creates an experience of catharsis and clarity. Wake up, have your coffee, grab your journal and copy of "Everyday Affirmations," and experience 365 days of positive change.

- Devyn

1

the thought

There are 86,400 seconds to start over each day -
do not limit yourself.
Your evolution is beautiful,
and your reinvention is your higher self,
reminding you of who you are.

the affirmation

I welcome and support my evolution.

the journal prompt

What is a simple thing that I can do today
to make my life feel more authentic?

2

the thought

Your power lies within you.
Difficult situations give you an opportunity
to acknowledge how capable you are.

the affirmation

I own my power fully & completely.

the journal prompt

When do I feel most powerful?

3

the thought

Fear does not prevent death; it prevents life.
Do not let your fear become
more prominent than it is meant to be.

the affirmation

I walk through life unafraid.

the journal prompt

When does my fear help me?
When does my fear hurt me?

the thought

When in doubt, give more love.

the affirmation

Regardless of external circumstances,
I lead with internal love.

the journal prompt

How do I show love, and how do I wish
others would show love to me?

5

the thought

You have an entire lifetime to figure it all out.
Stop doubting your journey
by confining yourself to manufactured timelines.

the affirmation

I have plenty of time.

the journal prompt

When have I let timelines dictate my actions?

6

the thought

Happiness is a byproduct of
high vibrational living.
The more time you spend in
gratitude, freedom, joy, empowerment,
and love, the happier you will feel.

the affirmation

I operate solely at my highest frequency.

the journal prompt

What does happiness feel like to me?

7

the thought

Gratitude is inherent.
You do not need to spend a lifetime proving
to yourself, or others, that you are
grateful or appreciative.

the affirmation

Gratitude naturally spills out of me.

the journal prompt

If I stopped looking outside of myself
for things to be grateful for,
what would my soul naturally appreciate?

8

the thought

Your body is simply a shell to protect your soul
and a vehicle to get you around this planet;
being obsessed with appearance
is old programming.

the affirmation

*I am so much more than how I appear
to the outside world.*

the journal prompt

What makes me glow from the inside out?

9

the thought

You have UNLIMITED amounts of love
to give. You lose nothing by saying,
"I love you" often.

the affirmation

I love freely and openly.

the journal prompt

When do I find myself feeling
afraid or hesitant to share my love?

10

the thought

When you approach things like they
are heavy, they will feel heavy.
All situations will carry your exact,
perceived burden.

the affirmation

I approach every situation with ease and light.

the journal prompt

What is something that I am dreading?
How can I approach it without the
heaviness of my thoughts?

11

the thought

Life is good when you allow it to be.

the affirmation

I welcome joy, love, and excitement.

the journal prompt

When do I feel the most excited about my life?

12

the thought
Your ego is trying to protect you,
but your soul is your ultimate guide.
Listen to the stirrings within you and allow
yourself to live from the inside out.

the affirmation
I trust my soul's guidance.

the journal prompt
When has my ego steered me wrong?
What would have been different about that
scenario had I listened to my soul?

13

the thought

Money is energy.

Start changing the word *money* to the word(s),

freedom or *peace*, and enjoy abundance.

the affirmation

I am abundant always, in all ways.

the journal prompt

What is my number one money fear and

why does it exist?

14

the thought

You have nothing to worry about; nothing
meant for you will pass you by.

the affirmation

Everything that is for me
is on its way to me, in perfect time.

the journal prompt

Why am I in such a rush?

15

the thought

You are built to come back from any
and all hardships.

the affirmation

I am incredibly resilient.

the journal prompt

What is my most incredible comeback story?

16

the thought

There is great beauty in recognizing
small moments of peace and soaking them up.

the affirmation

I exist in a continuous state of inner peace.

the journal prompt

When do I feel most at peace?

17

the thought

Sit in silence
with your thoughts and listen.
Stillness will grant you the ability to
find answers to all you seek.

the affirmation

I hear my inner voice loud and clear.

the journal prompt

When was the last time I was completely still?
Did I feel resistance?

18

the thought

Anything that you are chasing
is running away from you.
The less you force and the more you surrender,
the more magnetic you become.

the affirmation

I am a magnet for all things meant for me.

the journal prompt

What have I been chasing,
and do I believe it is meant for me?

19

the thought

When triggered by someone, ask yourself what
that is saying about you, not the other person.

the affirmation

I look inward to know what I need to work on.

the journal prompt

Who / what triggers me most and what
does that mean for my healing?

20

the thought

Your heart produces the most extensive
electromagnetic field of any organ.
You can detect this ECG on any body surface,
and it radiates up to five feet outside
your physical form, meaning that people
can feel you before seeing you.

the affirmation

*My heart chakra is free of all
energetic blockages.*

the journal prompt

How do I hope that others feel my energy?

21

the thought

Your greatest superpower is that you are you;
celebrate your authenticity and uniqueness.

the affirmation

I celebrate all parts of myself – I am unique.

the journal prompt

What is the most extraordinary thing about me?

22

the thought

Someday, everything you are going through
right now will make perfect sense.

the affirmation

*I believe that everyone and everything
is working for me, never against me.*

the journal prompt

What is one lesson I've learned from a
previously difficult time?

23

the thought

We must get to know ourselves to love
(and actually like) ourselves.

the affirmation

*I am committed to loving and liking myself
through understanding.*

the journal prompt

What is something I like about myself?

24

the thought

Life is only whole once we rid ourselves of
attachments to people, places, and things.
The goal is not hyper-independence,
the goal is to realize that we already
have everything we need.

the affirmation

I already have everything I need.

the journal prompt

What do I need to detach myself from?

25

the thought

A single emotion only lasts 90 seconds.
Our continuous thought about
said emotion makes us feel awful for days,
weeks, months, and even years.
Let feelings come and go as they are meant
to and have clarity in seconds.

the affirmation

*My mind, body, and soul process emotions
quickly and in perfect time.*

the journal prompt

What is an emotion that I've been holding
onto and am ready to let go of?

26

the thought

We rise by lifting others.
There is plenty of room for everyone
and no one else's success will have a
negative impact on yours.

the affirmation

I make room for others at the top.

the journal prompt

When do I feel jealous
of someone else's success and why?

27

the thought

There is no such thing as
right vs. wrong or good vs. bad.
There is what is right and good for you
vs. what is right and good for everyone else.

the affirmation

I love and accept myself and others.

the journal prompt

How has my judgment of others hurt me?

28

the thought

Acknowledging human duality is crucial.
There is no light without dark.

the affirmation

I suppress nothing.

the journal prompt

What is something I have been conditioned
to hide or suppress?

29

the thought

The good news and the bad news
is that everything is your fault.
You must praise yourself
for creating your dream life as often as
you doubt your decision-making.

the affirmation

I trust that all decisions I make are steps
in the right direction.

the journal prompt

What is one decision that I am genuinely proud of?

30

the thought

Your life changes when you get sick
and tired of being sick and tired.

the affirmation

I am capable of helping myself.

the journal prompt

What am I sick and tired of right now?

31

the thought

Only hurt people hurt people.

Have empathy and move forward with love.

the affirmation

I am the light when faced with darkness.

the journal prompt

How do I wish someone had treated me when
I was in a low or painful moment?

32

the thought

Believe in love because of the way you love.
Don't settle, don't get bitter, don't give up,
just be patient and be ready to receive.

the affirmation

I am open to the greatest love I can imagine.

the journal prompt

What are five things that I need in a
loving relationship?

33

the thought

Like attracts like.
Whatever is showing up in your life
(negative or positive) is a direct reflection
of the energy you emit to the world.

the affirmation

I choose to emit only good energy into the world.

the journal prompt

What is one thing I can do
to raise my vibration today?

34

the thought

You never have to hustle for your worth.
Performing, being busy, and other false societal
claims of measuring productivity end with you.
You are inherently worthy.

the affirmation

I am worthy and deserving of all good things.

the journal prompt

What is one thing I can do to stop trying
to prove my worth to others?

35

the thought

Unsubscribe.

Whether on social media or in real life,
remove people who make you feel less than
from your timeline and your world.

the affirmation

*I choose my company
and companionship wisely.*

the journal prompt

Who do I feel my best around?

36

the thought

Your trauma, your experiences, and
your hardships are all valid.
They do not, however, define you, nor do they
dictate the remainder of your journey.
Let it go.

the affirmation

I release what no longer serves me.

the journal prompt

Write a list of things/feelings/grudges
you are willing to let go of.

37

the thought

When you continue to do the same thing
over and over and expect different results,
you drive yourself insane.
Disrupt your routine.

the affirmation

*I welcome change and believe in the power
of new beginnings.*

the journal prompt

How can I shake up my daily routine?

38

the thought

You wouldn't have the vision
if it weren't yours.
Your dream life, ideas, thoughts, and manifestations
are exclusive to you and attainable.

the affirmation

My life keeps getting better and better.

the journal prompt

What does my dream life look like?

39

the thought

Love the lovers.
Surround yourself with unconditional love.

the affirmation

I welcome unconditional love.

the journal prompt

Write down five reasons why you love yourself
and five reasons why others love you.

40

the thought

Do not match someone else's energy.
Maintain your energy and attract people
who can meet you where you are.

the affirmation

My energy is sacred and cannot be diluted.

the journal prompt

Do I match other people's energy
(for better or worse)?

41

the thought

Be brave and try something new.
Being willing to get out of your comfort zone
will reward you every single time.

the affirmation

My growth is contingent upon going outside
of my comfort zone.

the journal prompt

What is something
that I have wanted to try forever?

42

the thought

We see everything through the lens of our
experiences, emotions, and attachments.
When you react strongly to something,
take a step back and see
the scenario from another perspective.

the affirmation

*I am not so attached to my perspective
that I cannot see another.*

the journal prompt

Whose lens would I like to see things through
to understand them better, and why?

43

the thought

Not being able to say "no" is a coping mechanism.
Creating healthy boundaries is crucial.

the affirmation

My boundaries keep my relationships healthy.

the journal prompt

Write a list of 20 things you want to say,
"no" to this year.

44

the thought

Depression is thinking about your past.
Anxiety is thinking about your future.
Gratitude is living in the present moment.

the affirmation

I am where I am supposed to be
at this very moment.

the journal prompt

When I look around,
what are three things I can see,
two things I can hear,
and one thing I can feel?

45

the thought

If you have time to overthink the worst-case scenario, you have that same amount of time to overthink the best-case scenario.

the affirmation

I trust that everything is working out for my highest good.

the journal prompt

What is my best-case scenario?

46

the thought

When you are tired, learn to rest.
Rest does not make you lazy or less valuable,
it restores your mind, your body, and your soul.

the affirmation

I honor my mind, body, and soul
when I am tired.

the journal prompt

What are ways that I can rest (other than sleep)?

47

the thought

Everything is an energy transfer.
If you are continuously doling out
energy and not getting anything back,
you will always feel depleted.

the affirmation

*I deserve the same amount of energy input
that I output daily.*

the journal prompt

What are three things that take energy from me?
What are three ways I can replenish?

48

the thought

Breathwork is the key to everything.

the affirmation

I breathe in positivity.
I breathe out what no longer serves me.

the journal prompt

What is my deep breathing mantra?

49

the thought

To be 'good' for everyone else,
you must put yourself first.
We cannot pour from an empty cup,
nor can we assume that people are going to
put our needs before their own.

the affirmation

*I love myself enough to know that self-care
is not selfish; it is necessary.*

the journal prompt

If I loved myself right now, what would I do?

50

the thought

Get your hopes up.
The power of positive thinking is real.

the affirmation

I am excited about the future.

the journal prompt

What am I most excited about when
I look to my future?

51

the thought

Emotional pain will turn into physical pain
if left unhealed.
Stare into the depths of your emotional wounds
and continue to do the work.

the affirmation

My emotional healing is my priority.

the journal prompt

What is the first emotional wound that needs
my attention?

52

the thought

Success is subjective.
Your success may look completely
different from someone else's.
Both are impressive,
and each person is of equal value.

the affirmation

I am valuable regardless of monetary success.

the journal prompt

What does ultimate success *feel* like to me?

53

the thought

You will have no regrets if you live each day
to the fullest and without
seeking validation from the outside world.

the affirmation

My life is perfect for me.

the journal prompt

When do I seek validation outside
of myself and why?

54

the thought

All of the things that have made you feel
like an outcast are the exact things that have
prepared you to live in your authenticity.

the affirmation

I choose my truth over being well-liked.

the journal prompt

What is something that I know to be true for me?

55

the thought

Walking away from things that are unhealthy for
you mentally, physically, and emotionally signals to
the universe that you are ready for an upgrade.

the affirmation

*I walk away from negative situations,
and I step into upgraded realities.*

the journal prompt

I feel healthiest (mentally, physically,
emotionally) when I do this one thing.

56

the thought

You are here to activate a specific group
of people. You cannot do so unless
you are willing to be heard. Speak up.

the affirmation

I clear my throat chakra by speaking my truth.

the journal prompt

When do I find myself staying silent?
What am I afraid of?

57

the thought

You do not need to explain yourself to anyone. Period.

the affirmation

I have peace in knowing exactly who I am.

the journal prompt

Do I find myself overexplaining my feelings?

58

the thought

Being afraid to experience complete joy is
depriving yourself of life's greatest pleasure.
We are built to live at a high vibration;
stop waiting for the other shoe to drop.

the affirmation

I welcome extreme joy and experience it in full.

the journal prompt

What is something
that I am genuinely joyful about?

59

the thought

You're not asking for too much;
you are just asking the wrong people.

the affirmation

I am unafraid to ask for what I deserve.

the journal prompt

What am I afraid to ask for in my life?

60

the thought

Be patient and live in the moment –
if you got everything right now,
where would you put it all?

the affirmation

*I have patience, knowing that I am
always on the right path.*

the journal prompt

What am I most looking forward to receiving?

61

the thought

The most spiritually awakened version of yourself lives beneath the programming and conditioning you have endured since birth. Strip everything away and reveal your soul.

the affirmation

I exist daily as my highest self.

the journal prompt

What does experiencing life as my highest self look like?

62

the thought

Take a look at your habits and ask whether or
not you are evolving or simply revolving.
You're never moving backward,
but you might be moving in circles.

the affirmation

*I practice daily habits that move me forward
and prepare me for the next phase.*

the journal prompt

What is a daily habit that I would like to eliminate?

63

the thought

Heal so that you don't sabotage everything
that is sent to help you.

the affirmation

I choose to see the world through a healed lens.

the journal prompt

What would it take for me to break
some of my walls down?

64

the thought

You must learn to be at home in your own body
to feel security.
Realize that you are your stability.

the affirmation

I am safe.

the journal prompt

Where/when do I feel most at home?

65

the thought

There is no need to apologize for wanting more.

the affirmation

I am worthy of taking up space in the world.

the journal prompt

Are my dreams big enough?
What would they look like x 10?

66

the thought

Understanding emotional intimacy will have you
teaching people how to love you correctly.

the affirmation

*I am unafraid to tell people who I am and
exactly what I need.*

the journal prompt

What do I need someone else to know
about me so they can love me fully?

67

the thought

Feel everything.

Feeling reminds us of our collective humanity.

All souls are connected

through our experiences and emotions.

the affirmation

I allow myself to feel everything.

the journal prompt

When do I find myself numbing my feelings?

68

the thought

Your manifestation journey includes action,
go after the big dreams.
The waiting game is a losing one.

the affirmation

I act on everything I believe in.

the journal prompt

What is one action step I want to take today?

69

the thought

Being soft-hearted is brave.
Sometimes trying softer works more
effectively than trying harder.

the affirmation

I keep my heart open and honor my vulnerability.

the journal prompt

When was there a time that trying softer
worked better for me?

70

the thought

What other people think and say about you
is none of your business.
If you base your feelings on the outside world's
opinions, you will lose yourself every time.

the affirmation

*My opinion of myself
is the only opinion that matters to me.*

the journal prompt

When do I feel most self-critical, and when
do I feel most self-celebratory?

71

the thought

When something negative tries to take over,
take away its only power: your time and attention.

the affirmation

I give my attention consciously.

the journal prompt

What do I want to focus my energy on today?

72

the thought

Stay close to people who feel like sunshine.
Their glow will remind you of yours,
their warmth will keep you from becoming cold
to the outside world, and their ability
to shed light on your darkness will help you heal.

the affirmation

I attract people who feel like sunshine.

the journal prompt

What are some traits that I admire in my
warmest friends and acquaintances?

73

the thought

One of the most powerful things you can do
is nothing at all.

the affirmation

I surrender.

the journal prompt

What do I need to surrender to the universe?

74

the thought

Loving others is easy when we realize
that we are all products of our pain.
Having felt any pain or discomfort in
your life is understanding
how easy it is to react from a place of hurt.

the affirmation

I forgive others quickly and easily.

the journal prompt

Who do I need to forgive?

75

the thought

It is not your job to fix
or re-parent anyone other than yourself.

the affirmation

I am who I always needed.

the journal prompt

If I ask my inner child what he/she/they needs,
the answer would be the following:

76

the thought

Time never moves backward, and neither do you.
Even when you feel like you are spiraling,
you are moving forward.

the affirmation

I am always effortlessly moving forward.

the journal prompt

Do I feel restricted by time?

77

the thought

Intentions are not enough.
Your words and actions must follow how
you intend to show up in the world.

the affirmation

My words and actions are thoughtful,
conscious, and aligned.

the journal prompt

What is my intention for today
and how do I plan to act on that?

78

the thought

Your work is necessary.
The world needs everything you produce,
and you will positively impact the planet by
doing exactly what you are doing right now.
Appreciate what you create.

the affirmation

My work is necessary, and my ideas are gold.

the journal prompt

What is my most significant
career/work-related goal?

79

the thought

It takes time to realize what is good for us,
but when we do, it is our responsibility
to eliminate anything else from our lives.

the affirmation

I choose what is good for me on every level.

the journal prompt

Make a list of 10 things that you have learned
are good for you.

80

the thought

Happy people quit.
Leave that job you hate,
stop doing things you don't feel like doing,
and end the toxic relationship.
Quit anything that feels out of alignment
with your highest self.

the affirmation

I quit everything that no longer aligns with me.

the journal prompt

If I am being honest with myself,
which part of my life expired a while ago?

81

the thought

Communication is the only thing that will take
your relationships from good to great.
We must speak to each other in a way that is honest,
non-judgmental, effective, and progressive.

the affirmation

I choose communication over silence.

the journal prompt

What is a conversation
that I have been putting off?

82

the thought

You will never know what you like or dislike
unless you experience many trials and errors.

the affirmation

I try everything to get to know myself better.

the journal prompt

What are three things that I'd really like
to try this month?

83

the thought

If you slow down and listen to your body,
it will always tell you exactly what you need.
It is on you to honor your needs.

the affirmation

I listen to my body and give it what it needs.

the journal prompt

What does my body need today?

84

the thought

As your world gets bigger,
your experiences get more complex.
Stay open to the lessons and keep space in
your heart to hear people's stories.

the affirmation

I am a great listener.

the journal prompt

What is the most interesting story I have
ever heard from a stranger?

85

the thought

Fun is a manifestation catalyst.
The more fun you have, the more quickly the
perceived impossible becomes possible.

the affirmation

I welcome copious amounts of fun.

the journal prompt

When do I find myself
having the most fun in my life?

86

the thought

Your soul doesn't suffer; your ego does.

the affirmation

My suffering is temporary.

the journal prompt

What is causing me to suffer right now?

87

the thought

The only thing holding you back is a
a blocked version of yourself.
When you remove emotional roadblocks,
the highway to everything you desire clears,
and you can get in the highspeed lane.

the affirmation

I release all emotional blockages
and break down all barriers.

the journal prompt

What is holding me back right now?

88

the thought

Getting clear about exactly what you want
will signal to the universe that you are ready
and willing to receive.
Be detailed and specific when manifesting.

the affirmation

I have total clarity; all fog has cleared.

the journal prompt

Getting as specific and detailed as possible:
what do I want?

89

the thought

Small steps are required to make giant leaps.
Making microscopic changes over time,
add up to significant results.

the affirmation

I can create positive change
in my everyday life.

the journal prompt

What is something small
that I can do to brighten my day?

90

the thought

The more you listen to your inner voice,
the louder it gets.
The louder it gets, the more intuitive you become.

the affirmation

I have all of the answers I need within me.

the journal prompt

When I get quiet, I hear the following:

91

the thought

Being indecisive is a waste of time.

You already know what to do,

trust your gut.

the affirmation

I make decisions quickly and without self-doubt.

the journal prompt

When do I feel most indecisivee, and why?

92

the thought

Guilt is not inherent.
Every time you feel guilty about anything,
know an external source causes it.
Ask yourself who and where
your guilt comes from, and then
energetically give it back to that source,
it does not belong to you.

the affirmation

*I refuse to feel guilty about how
I choose to live my life.*

the journal prompt

Where does my guilt come from?

93

the thought

People will project their insecurities and
fears onto you; it's not your problem.
Keep clapping for yourself and go bigger.

the affirmation

I am proud of myself.

the journal prompt

When was the last time I celebrated myself?
How did that feel?

94

the thought

Be who you want to attract,
and your people will show up.

the affirmation

I know that my people will find me at my best.

the journal prompt

What traits and characteristics do the people
I want to attract into my life possess?

95

the thought

You will never be able to control external
circumstances or feelings, but you will
always be able to manage your reaction
to what comes and goes.

the affirmation

*I am in control of the way I react
to the things I can't control.*

the journal prompt

What do I tend to do when big feelings come up?

96

the thought

Love is an eternal force; it transcends space
and time and is limitless in its pursuit.

the affirmation

I know that love is wherever I am.

the journal prompt

What does love *feel* like to me?

97

the thought

You are constantly guided in the right direction when listening to your soul.

the affirmation

I take risks according to my soul.

the journal prompt

What was a calculated risk that paid off for me?

98

the thought

Whatever you allow will continue.

the affirmation

*I do not settle for anything less
than what I deserve.*

the journal prompt

What is something I feel that I am
currently settling for?

99

the thought

It is okay to forgive and keep people
at a comfortable distance.
Your time, life, and world are precious;
not everyone gets to participate.

the affirmation

I respect my boundaries.

the journal prompt

What is something in my life that is sacred to me?

100

the thought

There is a 1 in 4 trillion chance that we are born
a human and you are here!
You are special, and not by accident.

the affirmation

I am supposed to be here.

the journal prompt

When do I feel that my life is most intentional?

101

the thought

There are no coincidences.
When you feel like something is perfectly in
place, space, and time, that is because it is.

the affirmation

My life is intentional.

the journal prompt

When is a time that all of the pieces of my life
fit together magically?

102

the thought

Not everything happens for a reason,
but everything has meaning.
Understanding will give you peace.

the affirmation

I am always able to see the lesson.

the journal prompt

What is one difficult situation that I now
realize taught me a lesson?

103

the thought

Worrying about the future is a waste of time.
There is no need to emotionally
experience something before it happens.

.

the affirmation

I worry less each day
because I trust the way that it all unfolds.

the journal prompt

What was something I was so worried about
that never ended up happening?

104

the thought

Let people live; you don't know when
you are interrupting their karma.

the affirmation

I live and let live.

the journal prompt

Whose narrative do I try to control
and need to let go of?

105

the thought

Show up every day for you.

Not for validation, not for celebration or praise,

but because your soul is shining through.

the affirmation

I show up for myself every day.

the journal prompt

How can I show up for myself today?

106

the thought

Burning the right bridge is liberating.
Sometimes the only way to move
forward is to leave people, places,
and situations in the past.

the affirmation

I leave negative people and situations in my past.

the journal prompt

When was a time that I burned a bridge
and felt liberated by it?

107

the thought

The universe doesn't want what is good for you;
the universe wants what is best for you.

the affirmation

I trust that the universe has my back.

the journal prompt

What is best for me right now?

108

the thought

You are never ahead; you are never behind,
you are always perfectly on time.

the affirmation

I am where I should be on my journey.

the journal prompt

In what area of my life do I feel
like I am perfectly on time?

109

the thought

You will always win when you move in love
and with an open heart and genuine intentions.

the affirmation

*My intentions are genuine
and I am open to all that life has to offer.*

the journal prompt

Who is the most genuine person I know, and
what positive traits do they possess?

110

the thought

As your life changes, so will your circle.
Not everyone is meant to stay in your life forever;
allow people to come and go organically.

the affirmation

I allow people to teach me the lessons
that I need to know.

the journal prompt

What is one relationship that taught
me an important lesson?

111

the thought

Focusing on the right things will have you
thinking clearly and feeling at peace.

the affirmation

*I choose to focus only on things that
move me forward.*

the journal prompt

What do I need to focus on today in particular?

112

the thought

When you run from the work,
you hide from the rewards.

the affirmation

I welcome the success
that comes from my hard work.

the journal prompt

When do I shy away from doing the hard work?

113

the thought

No one else is supposed to understand your calling.

the affirmation

I answer when I am called.

the journal prompt

What is something I feel called to do?

114

the thought

The best revenge is no revenge.
Move on, mind yours, and be happy.

the affirmation

I allow myself to move on in peace.

the journal prompt

Have I ever sought revenge?
What happened?

115

the thought

Holding onto people, places, and feelings
with such a tight grip
won't allow you to receive anything better.
Don't block new opportunities because you're
too attached to your comfort zone.

the affirmation

I open myself up to receiving more.

the journal prompt

What would it mean for me to get
out of my comfort zone?

116

the thought

Sometimes there is no support system.
There is no applause; there is no one to tell
you they are proud, it is just you, your grind,
and the things you believe are possible.

the affirmation

If I can see it, I can make it happen.

the journal prompt

What is something that I believe is possible
for myself, regardless of what others say?

117

the thought

You are inspiring people that you don't
even realize are watching you.

the affirmation

I always do me.

the journal prompt

I hope that when people see my journey,
they realize the following:

118

the thought

Get up! Beating yourself up when you fall
will just keep you on the ground longer.
Brush yourself off,
put your head up and keep going.

the affirmation

I refuse to beat myself up when I make mistakes.

the journal prompt

What is something that I always
beat myself up about?

119

the thought

Having patience with ourselves and others
is one of the most simplistic ways to show love.

the affirmation

*I practice patience with myself
and those around me.*

the journal prompt

When do I need to practice more patience?

120

the thought

Mastering life is learning to surf.
Sometimes you're paddling towards a peak,
sometimes you're riding a wave,
sometimes you crash, and sometimes you're just
sitting on your board, waiting for the next swell.
Learn to appreciate all moments in the
metaphorical water equally.

the affirmation

I ebb and flow with life.

the journal prompt

How can I become more fluid?

121

the thought

In moments of loneliness,
put your hand on your heart, feel it beating,
and know that you are an entire universe.

the affirmation

My heart is a gift.

the journal prompt

Do I recognize the pure power in existing?

122

the thought

Your spirit cannot be confined.

the affirmation

I let my spirit run wild and free.

the journal prompt

How can I create more freedom in my life?

123

the thought

Being an optimist is not about
being forcefully positive or delusional.
It is about being in a negative moment and
knowing something better is ahead.

the affirmation

I walk through life as an optimist.

the journal prompt

How do I think I would benefit from living
a more optimistic life?

124

the thought

We can't always see
what we're being protected from,
but those five minutes of traffic you had to sit
in might have meant you missed being
the one in the collision up ahead.

the affirmation

I trust that I am being constantly protected.

the journal prompt

Do I feel supported by a higher source?

125

the thought

Showing up as your whole self
means that all you need is for the people
around you to show up as themselves as well.

the affirmation

I show up so that others can too.

the journal prompt

I can best show up for the people
around me by doing these few things:

126

the thought

Don't be afraid to express emotions.
Tears will cleanse you,
speaking up will clear your throat chakra,
and acknowledging your dark thoughts
will set your soul free.

the affirmation

I know that vulnerability is my superpower.

the journal prompt

When was the last time I cried?
How did it feel?

127

the thought

Healing is not linear.
You will have amazing days, painful days,
mediocre days, and days that you can
barely get out of bed.
All days are necessary.

the affirmation

My healing process is unique to me and
every moment of it is necessary.

the journal prompt

Why do I feel like I need to speed up my healing?

128

the thought

You can plan your life away, or you can surrender.
Either way, the outcome is the same; the
latter journey is much more enjoyable.

the affirmation

*I know that there is more in store for me
than I can even imagine.*

the journal prompt

Show me how it gets better.

129

the thought

There is a difference between
connection and attachment.
Healthy relationships thrive on having
connection without reliance.

the affirmation

I rely on myself to meet my needs.

the journal prompt

What do I rely on myself for?
What do I rely on others for?

130

the thought

Society has a bad habit of celebrating materialism. However, your value cannot be calculated by how much you possess. Your value is inherent.

the affirmation

I am valuable.

the journal prompt

When do I feel most valuable? Is that healthy?

131

the thought

What is good for you will always
bring out the best in you, not the worst -
that's how you'll know.

the affirmation

I only accept what brings out the best in me.

the journal prompt

What is something that brings out the best in me?

132

the thought

Look back without regret.
If it could have been different, it would have been.

the affirmation

I appreciate the experiences that lead me here.

the journal prompt

What is something I regret, and how can I begin
to accept it as a positive part of my journey?

133

the thought

You need to have a 'why' attached to everything.

Want to lose weight? *Why?*

Want to fall in love? *Why?*

Want to make more money? *Why?*

Understanding why something is important

to you will guide you to the how.

the affirmation

I follow my why.

the journal prompt

What is my current why?

134

the thought

Do not underestimate your physical environment's
impact on your mental health.
A cluttered space is reflective of a cluttered mind.

the affirmation

*I keep my environment uncluttered
so that I can have clarity.*

the journal prompt

What physical space needs my attention today?

135

the thought

Create often and without abandon.

the affirmation

I create the world around me.

the journal prompt

What is my most incredible creation?

136

the thought

Confidence has nothing to do
with being better than anyone else.
Confidence is about knowing your worth so that
you can be a mirror for others to see their own.

the affirmation

*Knowing my worth gives me the ability to
have confidence in myself & others.*

the journal prompt

How do I non-verbally tell people I am confident?

137

the thought

Communication is key,
but comprehension is necessary.

the affirmation

I speak with the intent to connect.

the journal prompt

What is a conversation that resonated with me?

138

the thought

If you are thinking about a yellow car,
you are going to see a yellow car.
It's not magic; it's that what we focus
on manifests itself.
Focus on what you want to see.

the affirmation

I always see my manifestations come to life.

the journal prompt

What is something that I've spoken into existence?

139

the thought

Unconditional love doesn't mean that you put
up with everything and anything; it means that
you can meet a person where they are,
love them there, and then choose whether or
not you'd like to be a part of *their* journey.

the affirmation

I choose my friends and lovers wisely.

the journal prompt

What does unconditional love feel like to me?

140

the thought

Your subconscious brain is 60,000 times
more powerful than your conscious brain.
Make sure that you are filling it
with meaningful, loving thoughts.

the affirmation

My subconscious rules from a place of love.

the journal prompt

What is one of my most repetitive thoughts?
Is it helping me or hurting me?

141

the thought

The only people who will ever try
to talk you out of your dreams are the people who
are afraid of their own; stop listening to them.

the affirmation

I know that my dreams are attainable.

the journal prompt

What is something that I have been talked out of,
but wish I had done/pursued?

142

the thought

Diamonds form under pressure
and then are cut to be molded
into the perfect stone.
The pressure and pain you have been through
has only made you more amazing.

the affirmation

I turn my pain into purpose.

the journal prompt

How can I better handle pressure?

143

the thought

Our society promotes normalcy because it's easy,
not because you are meant to be *normal*.

the affirmation

I love living to the beat of my own drum.

the journal prompt

How do I celebrate my uniqueness?

144

the thought

Insecurity is not inherent.
We don't come out of the womb thinking,
"I hope the doctor doesn't judge my
naked body!" we are programmed.

the affirmation

I find my perceived flaws beautiful.

the journal prompt

Where do my insecurities come from
if they do not come from within me?

145

the thought

Forget about hustling; start aligning.
When you work from a place of purpose
and alignment, everything falls into place.

the affirmation

I align myself with work that feels purposeful.

the journal prompt

Can I feel the difference between when I am
hustling and when I am in alignment?

146

the thought

So far, you've survived 100% of your bad days.

the affirmation

I am built for this.

the journal prompt

What would my highest self do on a bad day?

147

the thought

Stop *shoulding* all over yourself.
If you wanted to, you would have.

the affirmation

I feel zero guilt about my decision-making.

the journal prompt

When was the last time I made a decision
that felt good to me?

148

the thought

The golden rule says to treat others how you would
like to be treated, not how others treat you.

the affirmation

*I treat everyone with the same love,
kindness and respect that I desire.*

the journal prompt

When was the last time I did something
from my heart, expecting nothing in return?

149

the thought

Feeling any emotion other than appreciation
is impossible when in a state
of pure gratitude.

the affirmation

I find myself in a constant state of gratitude.

the journal prompt

What single trait of mine
am I most grateful for right now?

150

the thought

Change is inevitable,
your response to change is up to you.

the affirmation

*I believe that all change brings me
closer to my highest self.*

the journal prompt

What do I need to do to switch things up?

151

the thought

Elevation requires separation.
Your journey is specific to you,
not everyone is going to understand it
or be able to keep up with you.

the affirmation

I am unafraid to elevate.

the journal prompt

When did I have to separate myself
from someone as I evolved?

152

the thought

Rather than asking people how their day was,
start asking how their heart is.
Small talk is dead.

the affirmation

I have significant conversations only.

the journal prompt

What are some small talk phrases/questions that
I want to eliminate from my conversations?

153

the thought

You are seen, you are heard, and you are loved.

the affirmation

I feel seen, heard, and loved.

the journal prompt

When do I feel most seen, heard, and loved?

154

the thought

Our fear of succeeding
often overrides our fear of failing.
If we got exactly where we wanted to be,
could we maintain it?
The answer is yes; start playing big.

the affirmation

*I am confident in my ability to maintain
all of the success that comes my way.*

the journal prompt

Am I afraid of succeeding?

155

the thought

Life doesn't get easier; you just get better.
The more experiences you have,
the more quickly you can deal
with anything that life throws at you.

the affirmation

I am getting stronger every day, in every way.

the journal prompt

How can I open myself up to
experience more today?

156

the thought

You are never going to have it all figured out –
just enjoy what is happening now.

the affirmation

I always know what I need to know.

the journal prompt

What is one thing I know for sure?

157

the thought

Rejection is redirection.
Everything that doesn't happen is equally
as important as what does happen.
All rejection is moving you forward,
you are never on the wrong path.

the affirmation

Rejection moves me in the right direction.

the journal prompt

When is a time that one door opened,
only because another door closed?

158

the thought

Self-awareness breeds humility.
Self-aware people apologize;
they listen before they speak, and they
are constantly improving.

the affirmation

I love getting to know myself,
so that I can begin shedding my ego.

the journal prompt

What is something that I can improve on today?

159

the thought

Constantly looking backward
is a literal pain in the neck.
Keep your eyes on the road ahead,
your next move is your most important.

the affirmation

I release my past and look forward to my future.

the journal prompt

What is my next move?

160

the thought

The only math you need to know:

time + consistency = success

the affirmation

I am consistent in how I show up for the world.

the journal prompt

When has consistency equaled success in my life?

161

the thought

The less you need, the more you have.
The simpler your surroundings,
the fewer materials you desire and
the more you possess.

the affirmation

I appreciate life's simplicity.

the journal prompt

What is an area of my life that I'd like to simplify?

162

the thought

You betray yourself every time you say,
yes to something you know is not for you.

the affirmation

I only say, yes to things that are right for me.

the journal prompt

When do I find myself agreeing to more
than I'd like to take on?

163

the thought

All we have are time and choices.
Your life revolves around time
and energy well spent - choose wisely.

the affirmation

I spend my precious time and energy wisely.

the journal prompt

What do I want to spend time on today?

164

the thought

Natural attraction is mental, physical, and spiritual.
You will not have to
compromise your light for the right person.

the affirmation

I welcome soulmate connections.

the journal prompt

What does being with my soulmate feel like?

165

the thought

Turn the volume down on negative people
and the volume up on the positive people
in your life, you control the dial.

the affirmation

*I choose to pay more attention to the people
in my life who lift me up.*

the journal prompt

Who is someone that I always feel
supported by and how?

166

the thought

Our souls know that we are not
meant to be ordinary.
We are meant to fulfill our purpose.

the affirmation

My purpose is extraordinary, and so am I.

the journal prompt

What do I think I am on this planet to do?

167

the thought

We overthink, over-stress, and overwork our brains until
we create problems that don't exist. Stop, sit, and listen.

the affirmation

I create solutions.

the journal prompt

When I listen to myself,
what does my soul tell me to stop stressing about?

168

the thought

The less miserable you are,
the less company you will have.

the affirmation

*I operate from a place of gratitude
rather than grievances.*

the journal prompt

What do I find myself complaining about?

169

the thought

Life is good when you are.
Taking care of yourself from the
inside out is non-negotiable.

the affirmation

*I make my mental and physical
health my priority.*

the journal prompt

What can I do today to put my mental and
physical health at the forefront?

170

the thought

Don't forget to thank yourself
for everything that you do for yourself.

the affirmation

I thank my mind, body, and soul
for being what I need at all times.

the journal prompt

What would I like to thank myself for today?

171

the thought

People will tell you exactly who they are,
all you have to do is listen.

the affirmation

I can manage my expectations
by listening to others.

the journal prompt

How can I better manage my expectations?

172

the thought

You are truly a force.
Everything that tried to destroy you
has only made you stronger.

the affirmation

I am UNSTOPPABLE.

the journal prompt

When do I feel most unstoppable?

173

the thought

Wanting someone else to make you happy
is like buying all of the ingredients
and then expecting the cake to bake itself.
Someone else can give you everything
you need, and your happiness still
requires work that only you can put in.

the affirmation

I put in the work to make myself happy.

the journal prompt

What is one thing I can do for myself today
that will genuinely make me feel happy?

174

the thought

If it costs you your peace, it is too expensive.

the affirmation

I choose peace
and infinite healing over everything else.

the journal prompt

What is getting too metaphorically expensive
for me to have in my life?

175

the thought

Restriction of any sort
implies that you feel guilt or shame…
both are heavy; put them down.

the affirmation

I experience pleasure without guilt.

the journal prompt

How can I reframe my guilty pleasures?

176

the thought

When there is no clear answer,
there are a million possibilities.

the affirmation

I look for opportunities and have many options.

the journal prompt

What are my current options?

177

the thought

Look to the birds in the sky; they ask for nothing, yet they are always provided for.

the affirmation

I am always provided for.

the journal prompt

When do I feel universal support?

178

the thought

Emotional unavailability signals that
you do not feel worthy of being loved
and supported in the ways that you deserve to be.

the affirmation

I am worthy of genuine love and support.

the journal prompt

Write a list of five ways that someone else can
best love and support you.

179

the thought

Less fear, more hope.

the affirmation

I am hopeful about every present situation.

the journal prompt

What does my fear hold me back from doing?

180

the thought

It is never about what you have or don't have,
it is about how you experience it.

the affirmation

*I experience everything through
the lens of gratitude and joy.*

the journal prompt

What is an experience that I would
like to have again?

181

the thought

Stand face to face with what you find when
you do the work on yourself.

the affirmation

*I bravely look every self-discovery
directly in the eye.*

the journal prompt

What is something that I have learned
about myself recently?

182

the thought

Your boundaries cannot be determined by
whether or not others will honor them.

the affirmation

I set healthy boundaries based on my needs.

the journal prompt

Are my current boundaries effective?

183

the thought

Focus on the daily habits that it takes to
accomplish the goal rather than the goal itself.

the affirmation

*I am aligned with my goals
and therefore, I am disciplined.*

the journal prompt

What habits do I need to incorporate into
my daily routine to achieve my goals?

184

the thought

Keeping things just to have them is unnecessary.

the affirmation

I get rid of what no longer brings me joy.

the journal prompt

What *stuff* no longer brings me joy?

Can I part with something today?

185

the thought

Never be afraid to take up space in the world.

the affirmation

I am worthy of being seen.

the journal prompt

What does it look like for me
to take up space on this planet?

186

the thought

Learn to accept everything as it arrives.
When it gets to you is when you are ready for it.

the affirmation

I am ready for whatever I receive today.

the journal prompt

How can I better react to both positive
and negative news?

187

the thought

Energy transfer is real.
Be mindful of who you let touch you.

the affirmation

I only engage with good, clear energy.

the journal prompt

What does good energy feel like to me?

188

the thought

Nothing is testing you.
You are consistently being allowed to show up
as you say you are willing to.

the affirmation

I always walk the walk.

the journal prompt

Am I actually who I say that I am/want to be?

189

the thought

Removing certain people, foods, and words
from your life can solve many problems.

the affirmation

*I remove all things that have the potential
to block me from my blessings.*

the journal prompt

What is no longer serving me?

190

the thought

You must believe it to see it.

the affirmation

I allow myself to dream boldly.

the journal prompt

What is something that I am actively
manifesting right now?

191

the thought

Some roads are meant to be traveled alone.

the affirmation

I am content with my own company.

the journal prompt

What is something I know I must do alone?

192

the thought

Make sure you aren't asking for directions
from people who have never been
where you are going.

the affirmation

I seek guidance from my soul.

the journal prompt

Do I feel lost?
How do I get back on track?

193

the thought

Your life is not coincidental.

the affirmation

I am meant to be.

the journal prompt

Do I feel like I am meant to be here?

194

the thought

There is nothing wrong with being sad.
Just like any other emotion,
this too shall pass.

the affirmation

I allow for a full range of emotions.

the journal prompt

Do I allow myself to feel sadness?
Why or why not?

195

the thought

Solitude gives you the opportunity
to get to know yourself better.

the affirmation

I know myself; therefore, I love myself.

the journal prompt

What happens when I sit still?

196

the thought

Before you react, take a moment to breathe and
set an intention for your reaction.

the affirmation

I take time to react to every external situation.

the journal prompt

What are three things I can do to slow
down my emotional reaction time?

197

the thought

It is sometimes harder to be a good person
with a good heart, but it is worth it.

the affirmation

I am a good person with a good heart.

the journal prompt

When does my heart feel the best?

198

the thought

Manifest abundance
and accept it when it arrives.
Money will only make you more of who you are.

the affirmation

I accept all abundance in my life.

the journal prompt

Do I fear the abundance that I ask for?

199

the thought

Your honesty invites others to give you
the honesty that you deserve.

the affirmation

I am honest in every situation,
regardless of the outcome.

the journal prompt

What have I not been honest about
and need to get off my chest?

200

the thought

Be patient while everything unfolds.

the affirmation

I am patient as I learn the lessons.

the journal prompt

Am I able to find the lesson in everything?

201

the thought

Part of the process is outgrowing
your unhelpful behaviors.

the affirmation

I adopt positive habits moving forward.

the journal prompt

What is one toxic trait that I need to outgrow?

202

the thought

Appreciating the valleys as much as you
celebrate the peaks puts you into flow.

the affirmation

I treat all moments equally.

the journal prompt

What were this week's peaks and valleys?

203

the thought

Not all relationships are meant to be mended.
Forgive in your heart and move on.

the affirmation

I forgive easily and move on in peace.

the journal prompt

What is one relationship that I am
done trying to make work?

204

the thought

Coming to the table full
means that you don't need anyone to feed you.

the affirmation

I fill myself up; everything else is a bonus.

the journal prompt

How do I fill myself up?

205

the thought

Do everything to prove yourself right,
not to prove others wrong.

the affirmation

Everything I do is to prove myself right.

the journal prompt

What is my proudest accomplishment?

206

the thought

Love others in their love language, not yours.

the affirmation

I am committed to loving others
in a way that they receive love.

the journal prompt

What is my partner's love language?
What about my closest
friends and family members?

207

the thought

If you find yourself giving
more energy than you are receiving,
take a step back and reevaluate.

the affirmation

*I recognize my output v. input
and I reevaluate as necessary.*

the journal prompt

When do I find myself consistently
giving more than I am receiving?

208

the thought

There is no such thing as an
over-saturated market.

Just go for it.

the affirmation

I believe that I can make anything work.

the journal prompt

What am I ready to go for?

209

the thought

Building the foundation of your life takes
time, hard work, and consistency.

the affirmation

I am the architect of my life.

the journal prompt

What can I do to build a stronger
foundation for myself?

210

the thought

Spoil your body with the positive attention
that it wants, needs, and deserves.

the affirmation

I am healthy and strong, and I love my body.

the journal prompt

When do I physically feel the strongest?

211

the thought

When anger arises, combat it with compassion.
We seldom know the whole story.

the affirmation

I combat anger with compassion.

the journal prompt

When has having compassion for someone else
helped me to get to know them better?

212

the thought

When you are feeling helpless or lost,
ask yourself what you can do for yourself,
not what others can do for you.

the affirmation

I cancel all feelings of helplessness.

the journal prompt

What can I do for myself?

213

the thought

Being *rich* means something
different for everyone; define your success.

the affirmation

I live a rich life.

the journal prompt

What does your rich life look like?

214

the thought

When you begin to negotiate your non-negotiables, you compromise your integrity.

the affirmation

I am full of integrity.

the journal prompt

What are five of my relationship non-negotiables?

215

the thought

Believing in yourself before anyone else
does allows you to move mountains.

the affirmation

I move mountains.

the journal prompt

I believe in myself for these reasons:

216

the thought

Flexing your creative muscle
will help you to get in touch with
your yin energy.

the affirmation

My creative energy surges through me.

the journal prompt

How do I best express my creativity?

217

the thought

Having a high EQ (emotional intelligence)
will serve you in ways
that having a high IQ cannot.

the affirmation

I increase my emotional intelligence every day.

the journal prompt

How can I increase and practice my
emotional intelligence daily?

218

the thought

Arguing with someone who is committed
to misunderstanding you
is a waste of your time and energy.

the affirmation

I choose to remove myself from
conversations that go nowhere.

the journal prompt

When do I feel most misunderstood?

219

the thought

If you are ready to compare yourself
to someone, you better be willing to compare
your entire life to their entire life.

the affirmation

I know that comparison is the thief of joy.

the journal prompt

Who do I find myself comparing my life to?

220

the thought

Loving yourself is knowing that your self-improvement is about getting yourself closer to who you are at your soul level.

the affirmation

I am who my soul knows me to be.

the journal prompt

What do I need to do today to get closer to my soul-level of living?

221

the thought

Don't underestimate your magic.

the affirmation

I make magic happen.

the journal prompt

When do I feel the most magical?

222

the thought

When you avoid or suppress your feelings,
they get stuck inside of you in a way they
were never meant to be in the first place.

the affirmation

I let my emotions move through me.

the journal prompt

What emotion do I have stuck
inside of me right now?
What would it take for me to release?

223

the thought

Focusing on the absence of anything
will make you feel like you never have enough.

the affirmation

I always have enough.

the journal prompt

How do I take myself out of a lack mentality?

224

the thought

You are never lost
on the path to returning to yourself.

the affirmation

I am my home.

the journal prompt

Where am I currently on my journey?
Where would I like to be a year from now?

225

the thought

Not being the same person you were
a year ago is proof
of your beautiful and necessary evolution.

the affirmation

I am proud of my evolution.

the journal prompt

How have I noticed myself
evolving over the last few months?

226

the thought

Daily routines are meant to make your life
easier; if you find that they are doing the
opposite, eliminate whatever is making
your life more difficult.

the affirmation

I incorporate joy into my daily routines.

the journal prompt

Do I feel more joyful when in routine?

227

the thought

Opportunity will present itself,
make sure that you are prepared.

the affirmation

*I am prepared to meet all opportunities
that are meant for me.*

the journal prompt

How can I best prepare myself for opportunity?

228

the thought

Easy is not always the goal.

the affirmation

I can do hard things.

the journal prompt

What is something that feels hard right now
but that I know I can handle?

229

the thought

You can do all of the dieting, exercising,
and obsessing you want,
if you are not mentally healthy,
nothing will change or feel better.

the affirmation

I know that my health is all-encompassing.

the journal prompt

What is one thing I can do today
to work on my mental health?
What is one thing I can do today
to work on my physical health?

230

the thought

Happy people aren't hating.

the affirmation

I use my happiness to spread love to others.

the journal prompt

How can I further eliminate
negative feelings towards others?

231

the thought

You can't compromise
your values for companionship.
The right person will be on the same page.

the affirmation

*I attract partners who see my value
and who have the same moral compass.*

the journal prompt

What kinds of people do I currently attract?

232

the thought

Take advantage of being able to relax
when you get the chance to.

the affirmation

I am moving at the exact right pace.

the journal prompt

Do I give myself enough time to relax?

233

the thought

Love is the universal language
and just like any other language, it takes practice
to learn and understand.

the affirmation

I practice love, compassion, and empathy often.

the journal prompt

Am I ever afraid to give love? Why?

234

the thought

Take inventory of who you allow to live
rent-free in your thoughts, then evict as necessary.

the affirmation

I am careful with who and what I give thought to.

the journal prompt

What needs to be evicted from my mental space?

235

the thought

Fitting in will make you miserable.
You are here to be you,
not to be a copy of everyone else.

the affirmation

I honor my individuality.

the journal prompt

What makes me an individual?

236

the thought

You must do at least one thing each day that
is solely for you and brings you true joy.

the affirmation

I create my own joy every day.

the journal prompt

How can I create more joy for myself today?

237

the thought

Experience is your teacher.

the affirmation

I welcome a multitude of experiences.

the journal prompt

What is something that I could have only
learned from having a specific experience?

238

the thought

Love is not meant to be difficult or painful.

the affirmation

I believe that love is pure and pleasant.

the journal prompt

How have I been programmed to understand love?

239

the thought

Once you decide to step into who you are,
miraculous things will happen.

the affirmation

I believe in and welcome miracles.

the journal prompt

What would change in my life if I decided
to step into who I truly am?

240

the thought

It's okay to distance yourself
from people you love.

the affirmation

*I respect myself enough
to take some space when I need to.*

the journal prompt

Do I listen to myself when it is time to
distance myself from certain people?

241

the thought

The external world is ever-changing.
You have to find calm within the chaos.

the affirmation

I go within to find the calm that I am seeking.

the journal prompt

What makes me feel calm in moments of chaos?

242

the thought

Being around different kinds of people
will expose you to the world.

the affirmation

*I open my world up to people
from all walks of life.*

the journal prompt

When was the last time I had a conversation
that exposed me to a different perspective?

243

the thought

Admitting that you are wrong is liberating.

the affirmation

I am unafraid to admit when I am in the wrong.

the journal prompt

Do I have a difficult time admitting
when I am wrong?

244

the thought

You are making a difference in the world,
just by being here.

the affirmation

I am always making a difference in the world.

the journal prompt

When do I feel that I am making
the biggest difference in the world?

245

the thought

Healing is not linear.
Take your time, be patient, and recognize
that you don't have to put yourself
on unrealistic timelines.

the affirmation

I heal everything in perfect time.

the journal prompt

How has my healing journey been thus far?

246

the thought

You cannot have deep connections with people
who are disconnected from themselves.

the affirmation

*I connect to myself so that I can better
connect the world around me.*

the journal prompt

When do I feel most connected to myself?

247

the thought

Meditation is not about ridding your mind
of thoughts, it is about making peace
with your thoughts and finding comfort in silence.

the affirmation

I welcome all of my thoughts at all times.

the journal prompt

Have I ever tried meditation?
What worked and what did not?

248

the thought

The sun always rises.

the affirmation

I know that every day is new.

the journal prompt

What would I like to leave behind today?
What would I like to begin again tomorrow?

249

the thought

You must celebrate your small wins.

the affirmation

I celebrate myself often.

the journal prompt

Do I feel like I'm worthy of celebration?

250

the thought

Some people will never
be able to enjoy you because your spirit
aggravates their shadow…that's okay.

the affirmation

I am not for everyone,
and I am at peace knowing that.

the journal prompt

Why do I want to be well-liked by everyone?

251

the thought

You are growing through
what you are currently going through.

the affirmation

I grow in the face of adversity.

the journal prompt

Where can I see the most growth in my life
over the last five years?

252

the thought

When your mind is unsettled,
your body responds
with heightened cortisol levels.
You must remind your body
that you are okay for it to believe that you are.

the affirmation

I am okay.

the journal prompt

What causes me to feel unsettled in my life?

253

the thought

Self-deprecation is a coping mechanism.
How you speak about yourself is how you
feel about yourself.

the affirmation

*I speak kindly about myself
and I accept compliments from others.*

the journal prompt

How would I describe myself to someone
that I have never met before?

254

the thought

Focusing on your strengths creates opportunity.

the affirmation

I focus on my strengths.

the journal prompt

What are some of my strengths?

255

the thought

It is not hard to just be nice.

the affirmation

I spread kindness daily.

the journal prompt

What is something kind
that I can do for someone else today?

256

the thought

Confidence is controlling your inner dialogue.

the affirmation

*I override negative thoughts
about myself with empowering ones.*

the journal prompt

When do I feel most empowered?

257

the thought

You are never too young,
nor are you too old to try something new.
Your soul knows no age, only wisdom.

the affirmation

My soul dictates my next move.

the journal prompt

If age weren't a factor, what would I be doing?

258

the thought

Keep the promises you make to yourself.
Building trust between your mind, body, and spirit
is the foundation of everything else in your life.

the affirmation

I keep my promises to myself.

the journal prompt

What is a promise that I am willing to
make to myself (and keep) this year?

259

the thought

Acknowledge your talents
so that you can begin to cultivate a skillset.

the affirmation

I have a diversified skillset.

the journal prompt

Do I believe that I am talented?
How can I foster that talent?

260

the thought

Respond to inconsistency with unavailability.

the affirmation

I am unavailable for inconsistent people.

the journal prompt

When do I need to make myself less available?

261

the thought

Even when you can't see it,
everything is working in your favor; trust it.

the affirmation

I have faith in my future.

the journal prompt

What can I surrender to today?

262

the thought
Someone's life is better because you are in it.

the affirmation
I am a great friend.

the journal prompt
What makes me a great friend?

263

the thought

The more in touch with your mind you are,
the more in touch with your body you will be.

the affirmation

I am in complete mind-body alignment.

the journal prompt

What has my mind been telling my body lately?

264

the thought

We either feel overwhelmed
when faced with uncertainty,
or we welcome endless possibilities.

the affirmation

I welcome endless possibilities.

the journal prompt

What am I overwhelmed by currently and
how can I turn that into excitement?

265

the thought

Be at peace with not knowing everything.

the affirmation

I have all the information
that I need in this moment.

the journal prompt

What do I need to be at peace with right now?

266

the thought

Your gifts will flow through you in a way that
is both foreign and yet, deeply familiar.

the affirmation

My gifting and purpose are inherent.

the journal prompt

What area of my life do I feel most
naturally gifted in?

267

the thought

Give love to others when you need it most.

the affirmation

I give love when I want to feel love.

the journal prompt

When was the last time
that I wanted to feel someone else's love?

268

the thought

Pay attention to who your nervous system
feels good around.

the affirmation

*I surround myself with people who
add tremendous value to my life.*

the journal prompt

Who adds the most value to my life right now?

269

the thought

There is no such thing as original thought.
We are all constantly borrowing from each other,
learn to collaborate.

the affirmation

I share my wisdom,
thoughts and ideas with others.

the journal prompt

What is one thought or idea
that I can share to help other people?

270

the thought

The heart knows.

the affirmation

I listen to my heart.

the journal prompt

When have I listened to my heart
and have been led in the right direction?

271

the thought

Don't allow the bare minimum to impress you.

the affirmation

I am worth maximum effort.

the journal prompt

From whom do I currently accept
the bare minimum?

272

the thought

Sometimes smiling is just practice
for when you feel genuinely happy.

the affirmation

My smile brightens my day.

the journal prompt

Make a list of things that make you smile.

273

the thought

No one is coming to save you.

the affirmation

I am the savior I have been seeking.

the journal prompt

What is something that I can take off my plate
to help myself today?

274

the thought

Interrupt your negative thoughts
and replace them with positive ones.

the affirmation

I interrupt all negative thoughts.

the journal prompt

What empowering phrase can I use to
interrupt my negative thoughts?

275

the thought

Heal by facing the issue and releasing it.

the affirmation

I face it all so that I can release it all.

the journal prompt

What can I peacefully release today?

276

the thought

You are resilient.

the affirmation

I always get back up.

the journal prompt

When have I had to be resilient?

277

the thought

Keeping the peace outside of yourself will
only disrupt the peace within you.

the affirmation

*I keep the peace within myself before I worry
about keeping the peace outside of myself.*

the journal prompt

How do I keep the peace within myself?

278

the thought

Pause and enjoy the moment.

the affirmation

I take time to stop and smell the roses.

the journal prompt

What are three wonderful things
about this present moment?

279

the thought

You can't do epic things by being basic.
Challenge societal norms.

the affirmation

I challenge societal norms
and do extraordinary things.

the journal prompt

What is something that is considered
'normal,' but that I am uninterested in?

280

the thought

Instead of saying, *I don't have enough time,*
start saying *this isn't a priority*
and see how that feels.

the affirmation

I prioritize what is important to me.

the journal prompt

What is my priority today?
How about this week?

281

the thought

Your standards are never too high.

the affirmation

I know what I deserve, and thus, I expect it.

the journal prompt

What are my standards?

282

the thought

Unhelpful programming no longer serves you,
even if it feels familiar to you.

the affirmation

I am de-programmed.

the journal prompt

What is something that feels familiar to me
but that is not necessarily helpful?

283

the thought

Your truth will set you free.

the affirmation

I find freedom in my truth.

the journal prompt

What would it feel like to be fully honest
with myself and with others?

284

the thought

Everything you want is on the other side
of discipline and consistency.

the affirmation

*I respect myself enough to be disciplined
so that I can get to the next level.*

the journal prompt

What is my relationship with discipline?

285

the thought

Making money isn't hard,
placing proper value on money is.

the affirmation

Money flows to me because I understand
why it is important to me.

the journal prompt

Why is having money vital to me?

286

the thought

Take a break so that you don't.

the affirmation

I honor my mind and body enough
to take breaks when necessary.

the journal prompt

What do I need to take a break from currently?

287

the thought

Love yourself like you love others.

the affirmation

I love me, and so I love them.

the journal prompt

Does self-love/care feel selfish to me?

288

the thought

Your experiences determine the lens
through which you see the world.
Different people have different experiences -
have empathy for all.

the affirmation

*I have empathy for people who see
things differently than I do.*

the journal prompt

What does having empathy for others mean to me?

289

the thought

It is time to forgive yourself.

the affirmation

I forgive myself.

the journal prompt

What do I need to forgive myself for?

290

the thought

You are so much closer to
reaching that goal than you think you are.

the affirmation

I will keep going.

the journal prompt

What is my current goal?

291

the thought

If you want different,
you have to do things differently.

the affirmation

I cancel old habits
and welcome change within myself.

the journal prompt

In which area of my life
do I need to begin taking a different approach?

292

the thought

Focusing on quality over quantity,
in every situation will fulfill you.

the affirmation

I choose quality over quantity, always.

the journal prompt

When does less feel like more?

293

the thought

Being misunderstood might make you feel
temporarily alone but being inauthentic
to make other people comfortable will
make you feel permanently lonely.

the affirmation

I am always at home with my authentic self.

the journal prompt

Can I differentiate between being alone
and feeling lonely?

294

the thought
You never have to feel guilty about
experiencing happiness.

the affirmation
I enjoy all of life's pleasures.

the journal prompt
Do I allow myself to experience happiness fully?

295

the thought

The only regret we have is about the things we didn't say.

the affirmation

I speak with intention.

the journal prompt

What is something I wish I had said?

296

the thought

You will not meet anyone by accident.

the affirmation

*I know that all people come into my life for
a reason, a season, or a lifetime.*

the journal prompt

Who is someone that I believe is/has been
in my life for a specific reason?

297

the thought

You can't ignore your feelings.

the affirmation

I consider my feelings.

the journal prompt

What has my heart been telling me?
Have I been ignoring it?

298

the thought

Feeling underappreciated will have you
making a martyr of yourself.

the affirmation

I go where I am appreciated.

the journal prompt

When do I feel most appreciated
for being exactly who I am?

299

the thought

Mental health is real.

the affirmation

I prioritize my mental health.

the journal prompt

What is the best thing I have done
for my mental health recently?

300

the thought

Having a hard conversation is always worth it.

the affirmation

I am comfortable having difficult conversations.

the journal prompt

What was the last difficult conversation
I had to have, and how did it go?

301

the thought

Don't let other people tell you what is real for you.
Your feelings are valid.

the affirmation

I validate myself.

the journal prompt

Do I ever look inward for validation?

302

the thought

The universe will continue to give you the exact same lesson until you master it.

the affirmation

I am the master of my life.

the journal prompt

What is one lesson that I have mastered?

303

the thought

Don't be so busy working on things outside
your control that you forget to live.

the affirmation

I live fully.

the journal prompt

What would make my life feel whole?

304

the thought

All it takes is a feeling.

the affirmation

I am in tune with my inner guide.

the journal prompt

What just *feels* right in my life?

305

the thought

Your life, your choices.

the affirmation

I choose me, every time.

the journal prompt

What is a choice I have made solely for myself?

306

the thought

Sometimes the healing hurts more than the wound.

the affirmation

I know that my healing
will lead to lifelong happiness.

the journal prompt

Does time heal all?

307

the thought
Your subconscious brain
sends your body signals before your conscious
brain can fully process your feelings.

the affirmation
I trust my subconscious feelings.

the journal prompt
Do I trust the energy that I receive?

308

the thought

You are never a disappointment.

the affirmation

I am a success.

the journal prompt

What is my success story?

309

the thought

Stay close to whoever brings out the best in you.

the affirmation

I stick with people who see my light.

the journal prompt

When do I feel most understood, loved,
and appreciated?

310

the thought

If you aren't happy by yourself,
you won't be satisfied with a partner.
Relationships are not a solution to your
problems; they are an addition to your life.

the affirmation

My happiness comes from within.

the journal prompt

Have my romantic partners added value to my life?

311

the thought

Nothing will kill you like your mind.

the affirmation

My positive thinking shapes my reality.

the journal prompt

What do I do when I need to shift my
thoughts from negative to positive?

312

the thought

Separate your coping from your celebration.
You cannot fully heal
when you don't know the difference between
what feels good to you
and what you are trying to numb.

the affirmation

I have healthy coping mechanisms.

the journal prompt

How do I cope? How do I celebrate?

313

the thought

Trust when new people are introduced and trust
when other people remove themselves.

the affirmation

*I trust that the right people
will always come into my life.*

the journal prompt

Do I tend to hold onto relationships
past their expiration date?

314

the thought

It is not about doing; it is about *being*.

the affirmation

I allow my natural state of being to be enough.

the journal prompt

Who would I be if I stopped trying to do so much and just allowed myself to be?

315

the thought

Be open to pleasant surprises.

the affirmation

I am pleasantly surprised by life.

the journal prompt

When was the last time that I experienced
an enjoyable surprise?

316

the thought

Solitude has the words,
so lit in it because taking time to rejuvenate
alone sets your soul on fire.

the affirmation

I rejuvenate in solitude.

the journal prompt

How comfortable am I with solitude?

317

the thought

Visualize your highest self and then reverse
engineer your life from there.

the affirmation

I see my future.

the journal prompt

What is one step I can take today
that will get me closer to my vision?

318

the thought

Life is more fulfilling for the givers
than it is for the takers.

the affirmation

*I am fulfilled by giving my time and energy
to those who need and appreciate it.*

the journal prompt

When does giving feel better than taking?

319

the thought

Failure is simply your First Attempt In Learning.

the affirmation

Failure only ever moves me forward.

the journal prompt

When was the last time that my failure
moved me in the right direction?

320

the thought

Let go of residual anger
so that you can see the situation clearly.

the affirmation

I let go of residual anger so that I can have clarity.

the journal prompt

What is my instinct when anger arises?

321

the thought

Being self-critical is a waste of time.

the affirmation

I am done criticizing myself.

the journal prompt

What am I overly self-critical about?

322

the thought

Have compassion for yourself.

the affirmation

I have compassion for myself.

the journal prompt

How can I be more compassionate
towards myself in times of need?

323

the thought

Be bold in your decision-making.

the affirmation

I am confident that I always
make the right decisions for me.

the journal prompt

What is the boldest decision I've ever made?

324

the thought

If you constantly find yourself
feeling like nothing you ever do is enough,
you need to find different people.

the affirmation

I am inherently enough.

the journal prompt

Do the people I surround myself with make
me feel like a better version of myself?

325

the thought

What you think, you become.

the affirmation

I create my reality and
am becoming more of who I truly am every day.

the journal prompt

Have I created a reality for myself that I enjoy?

326

the thought

Permit yourself to let go of things that are
out of your control.

the affirmation

I fully release what I cannot control.

the journal prompt

When do I find myself wanting to be in control?

327

the thought

Inhale confidence, exhale self-doubt.

the affirmation

I have unlimited confidence.

the journal prompt

When do I doubt myself, and why?

328

the thought

When you feel disconnected from your loved ones, remember that you were born into an environment meant to teach you.

the affirmation

I am surrounded by people who show me more of who I am through life lessons.

the journal prompt

What has my family taught me?

329

the thought

Impact the lives of others by adding value.

the affirmation

I add value to my life and the lives of many.

the journal prompt

How do I add value to myself
and how can I add value to others?

330

the thought

Observe without judgment.

the affirmation

I observe others and then decide whether or not I'd like to be a part of their journey.

the journal prompt

When do I find myself being judgmental?

331

the thought

Don't worry if you are the only one.
Real is rare.

the affirmation

I am okay with being in my lane,
if it means that I get to be authentic.

the journal prompt

When do I feel like I am being
my most authentic self?

332

the thought

Love knows no distance or time.
If you are meant to be, you will be.

the affirmation

I trust that love will be what it is meant to be.

the journal prompt

Do I believe in *perfect* or imperfect timing
when it comes to relationships?

333

the thought

The goal is not to become cold
to the outside world,
the goal is to become unbothered by
people and their opinions of you.

the affirmation

I am living the most unbothered life.

the journal prompt

How can I keep my heart open without allowing
other people's opinions to affect me?

334

the thought

Don't rush your transformation.
All good things take time,
all great things take longer.

the affirmation

I transform in perfect time.

the journal prompt

What does transformation mean to me?

335

the thought

If you knew the magnitude of your power,
you would not be afraid.

the affirmation

I know my power and, therefore,
I know that I can handle anything.

the journal prompt

How can I use my internal power
to overcome my external fears?

336

the thought

Staying in the moment will bring you peace,
as it is the only moment that truly exists.

the affirmation

I exist in this moment.

the journal prompt

What does my present moment *feel* like?

337

the thought

Being tired is not the same thing as being weak.

the affirmation

I listen to myself and rest when necessary.

the journal prompt

What do I need to do to ensure
that I am feeling well-rested today?

338

the thought

Normalize leaving places when the vibe is off.

the affirmation

I trust my gut and I remove myself
from situations, without hesitation.

the journal prompt

Do I feel confident in my ability to act
when something doesn't feel right?

339

the thought

To address the problem,
you need to understand it.

the affirmation

*I seek knowledge and understanding
so that I can face every problem head-on.*

the journal prompt

Do I feel like I can see all sides of an issue?

340

the thought

Empowering others will empower you.

the affirmation

I empower others because I am empowered.

the journal prompt

How can I empower others?

How can I empower myself?

341

the thought

Don't underestimate the impact of simplicity.
Sipping water, taking a deep breath,
or just sitting by yourself
for a minute can be groundbreaking.

the affirmation

I value simplicity.

the journal prompt

What are some effortless ways
that I can make myself feel good right now?

342

the thought

Normalize setting boundaries upon first meetings.

the affirmation

I set healthy boundaries
at the beginning of all relationships.

the journal prompt

What is one boundary that I want to
begin every relationship with?

343

the thought

Sit with purpose-driven people,
the conversation is different.

the affirmation

I hang out with people who fit my future.

the journal prompt

When do I feel like I am in the presence
of people whom I admire?

344

the thought

Consciousness is the new sexy.

the affirmation

I feel my best when I am being conscious,
self-aware and mindful.

the journal prompt

Do I feel like I am self-aware?

345

the thought

The goal is to spend your days as you wish.

the affirmation

*I focus on being able to spend my days doing
what I want to do and when I want to do it.*

the journal prompt

How do I wish to spend my days?

346

the thought

Punishing yourself for a time when you
didn't know any better is self-sabotage.

the affirmation

*I forgive myself for all of the things
I did not know at the time.*

the journal prompt

What is something that I continue
to punish myself for…can I let that go?

347

the thought

Some people will love you, others will not,
and none of it will matter.

the affirmation

I am who I am, and I love it here.

the journal prompt

How much time do I spend thinking about
how other people feel about me?

348

the thought

You don't have to be perfect in order
to help other people.

the affirmation

I lend my experience to help others.

the journal prompt

How am I best at helping others through both
my negative and positive life experiences?

349

the thought

When nothing is going right, go left.

the affirmation

I pivot with ease because I am in my purpose.

the journal prompt

When has pivoting from one thing to another
helped me discover something I enjoy?

350

the thought

You are not too sensitive because you have emotional reactions to disrespect.

the affirmation

I am comfortable with my emotions and thus, have no reason to suppress them.

the journal prompt

When have I been told that I am overreacting, and how has that affected how I show emotion?

351

the thought

Ignite the light that is inside of you
by doing things that you love.

the affirmation

I make time for things that I love.

the journal prompt

What are five things that I love to do?

352

the thought

Savor your experiences.

the affirmation

I savor my time and cherish all of my experiences for exactly what they are.

the journal prompt

What experiences do I find myself savoring?

353

the thought

Give to others what you would like to receive.
The more positive, big-hearted energy you put
into the world, the more you will get back.

the affirmation

I am generous with my time, energy, care, etc.
and believe I deserve the same in return.

the journal prompt

What do I believe I deserve?

354

the thought

There is no final destination.

the affirmation

I evolve, grow, and transform with ease.

the journal prompt

Do I leave room in my life for continuous growth?

355

the thought

Confidence is not hoping that they like you,
confidence is knowing
that you are okay if they don't.

the affirmation

*My confidence comes from knowing
my worth and loving myself.*

the journal prompt

In which area of my life am I most confident?

356

the thought

You are under no obligation to be the same
person you were even a second ago.

the affirmation

I allow myself to change my mind.

the journal prompt

When was the last time I changed my mind
about something significant?

357

the thought

Reflect deeply and often.

the affirmation

I hold space for reflection.

the journal prompt

What do I find out about myself
when I make time for reflection?

358

the thought

There are people and places that benefit
solely from being in your presence.

the affirmation

My presence is a present.

the journal prompt

When can I feel my presence making an impact?

359

the thought

Happiness cannot be bought, sold, or traded.

the affirmation

My happiness is determined by what I am.

the journal prompt

Am I waiting for something outside of myself
to make me happy?

360

the thought

Your beliefs are just as important as your behavior.
Make sure that the two align.

the affirmation

My beliefs and my behavior fully align.

the journal prompt

What are my beliefs, and does my
behavior align with those beliefs?

361

the thought

Tough times don't make you stronger,
they remind you that you already are.

the affirmation

I can handle anything.

the journal prompt

When am I able to harness my strength?

362

the thought

Don't wait for inspiration; seek it.

the affirmation

The world around me inspires me.

the journal prompt

What is my greatest inspiration?

363

the thought

It is not worth it to spend
one more minute at war with yourself.
You are your greatest ally.

the affirmation

The war is over; I am at peace with myself.

the journal prompt

What battle do I need to end with myself?

364

the thought

Love is a verb: choose it, be it, act on it.

the affirmation

I choose love; I am love, I give love.

the journal prompt

How can I be *love* today?

365

the thought
You are the entire universe.
PLAY BIG!

the affirmation
I am the universe.

the journal prompt
What do I need to do to play big?

I love you.

Devyn Penney is a certified international life coach and author. A born entrepreneur and thought leader, Devyn has spent her career teaching confidence, connection, and helping people re-discover their authenticity. She has worked with clients worldwide, providing resources that allow them to get to know themselves better, love themselves more, and empower them to live lives full of purpose and peace. When she is not on a client call or writing her next book, Devyn enjoys weekly exercise classes, reading the latest self-development best seller, and discovering new things to do in her New York City neighborhood.

For more information about how to work with Devyn, please visit **www.devynpenney.com.**

CPSIA information can be obtained
at www.ICGtesting.com
Printed in the USA
BVHW040804160223
658141BV00018B/54